Many plans are in

a person's mind,

but the Lord's purpose

will succeed.

Proverbs 19:21 (CEB)

Endorsements

In these pages, your church leaders are invited to quality time with a seasoned ministry development guide. Ken Willard has walked with hundreds of churches down the road of helping them clarify what on earth they seeking to do and why they care enough to do it. The longer your church has been around, the more likely you are flying on autopilot and steadily losing altitude. Ken Willard can help your church soar again."

Paul Nixon
Author, *Cultural Competency*
Co-Author, *Launching a New Worship Community*

Global and local disruptions of varied scales, sorts and speeds are the new normal. When life is disruptive, it is essential that churches are clear about and focused on their unchanging mission to make disciples of Jesus Christ, their world-transforming purpose, and their vision for the difference they can make in their communities. I highly recommend this practical, action-oriented book as a resource for churches seeking clarity about what Christ calls them to do, why it's important to do it, and the vision of where they are going.

Bishop Ruben Saenz, Jr.
Great Plains Conference of The United Methodist Church

The What, Why & Where is a handy guide for you and your team to begin listening to the Holy Spirit's direction for the next season of your church's ministry.

Amy Shanholtzer
Dean of the Cabinet, West Virginia Conference of The United Methodist Church

Meaning matters! In this newest addition to the Greatest Expedition series, Ken Willard guides congregational leaders in their journey of claiming missional purpose. I especially recommend his excellent Church Self Study resource in *The What, Why, & Where* as a practical roadmap for churches seeking to find their way in this challenging new season of ministry.

Blake Bradford

Co-author of *Mission Possible: A Simple Structure for Missional Effectiveness*

Ken Willard has offered a gift to the church in this text. This is the resource for the church that knows it needs a renewed direct but is not sure where to start. I will definitely be using this resource to engage congregations as they begin the adventure of transformation and renewal.

Aaron M. Bouwens

Director of Vital Congregations, Upper New York Conference of The UMC

I am a Ken Willard fan. He has, once again, produced a well-researched and thought-provoking book. If your church is struggling to find vision and clarity for the future, open these pages. Within them, you will find the tools necessary to discover focus and purpose in your ministry. I highly recommend it to you.

Ken Nash

Lead Pastor of Cornerstone Church, Grand Rapids, Michigan

THE WHAT,
What is it we do? (Mission)

WHY &
Why do we do it? (Purpose)

WHERE
Where is God calling us? (Vision)

Ken Willard

THE WHAT, WHY & WHERE
of the New Expedition

©2021 Ken Willard

books@marketsquarebooks.com
141 N. Martinwood Rd. Knoxville TN 37923
ISBN: 978-1-950899-39-5

Printed and Bound in the United States of America
Cover Illustration & Book Design ©2021 Market Square Publishing, LLC

Contributing Editor: Kay Kotan

All rights reserved. No part of this book may be reproduced in any manner without written permission except in the case of brief quotations included in critical articles and reviews. For information, please contact Market Square Publishing, LLC.

**Unless noted, Scripture quotations taken from
the CEB version of the Holy Bible:**

CEB

Scripture quotations marked (CEB) are taken from the Common Bible: New Revised Standard Version Bible. Copyright ©1989 by the Division of Christian Education of the National Council of the Churches of Christ in the United States of America. Used by permission. All rights reserved.

MSG

Scripture quotations marked MSG are taken from THE MESSAGE, copyright © 1993, 2002, 2018 by Eugene H. Peterson. Used by permission of NavPress, represented by Tyndale House Publishers. All rights reserved.

This resource was commissioned as
one of many interconnected steps in the
journey of *The Greatest Expedition*.

GreatestExpedition.com

Table of Contents

Foreword 1
By Kay Kotan

Introduction 3
What, Why & Where?

Chapter One 7
Mission

Chapter Two 33
Purpose

Chapter Three 41
Vision

Chapter Four 61
Church Life Cycle

Afterword 65
Leadership is Hard Work

Appendix

    Additional Books 69

    Church Self-Study 73

        Section One – History 74

        Section Two – Statistics. 77

        Section Three – Community Study. 80

        Section Four – Demographics. 82

        Section Five – Documents 86

        Section Six – Discipleship 88

        Section Seven – Questionnaire 89

        Section Eight – Leadership Questions ... 94

Acknowledgments 97

Foreword

This resource was commissioned as one of many interconnected steps in the journey of *The Greatest Expedition*. While each step is important individually, we intentionally built the multi-step Essentials Pack and the Expansion Pack to provide a richer and fuller experience with the greatest potential for transformation and introducing more people to a relationship with Jesus Christ. For more information, visit GreatestExpedition.org.

However, we also recognize you may be exploring this resource apart from *The Greatest Expedition*. You might find yourself on a personal journey, a small group journey, or perhaps a church leadership team journey. We are so glad you are on this journey!

As you take each step in your expedition,

your Expedition Team will discover whether the ministry tools you will be exploring will be utilized only for the Expedition Team or if this expedition will be a congregational journey. Our hope and prayer is *The Greatest Expedition* is indeed a congregational journey, but if it proves to be a solo journey for just the Expedition Team, God will still do amazing things through your intentional exploration, discernment, and faithful next steps.

Regardless of how you came to discover *The Greatest Expedition,* it will pave the way to a new God-inspired expedition. Be brave and courageous on your journey through *The Greatest Expedition!*

Kay L Kotan, PCC
Director, *The Greatest Expedition*

INTRODUCTION
What, Why & Where?

"So, what do you do?"

"Where are you going?"

Imagine your Greatest Expedition is taking you across the country. You and the whole Expedition Team will need to take several flights to your destination. On one of the flights, you find yourself in an airplane seat away from the rest of your team during your trip. You are sitting next to someone you have never met before. You want to be friendly, so you casually introduce yourself. They smile, introduce themselves, and then ask those two questions listed at the beginning. The two most common questions frequent travelers have heard for many years when crossing paths with someone new. "What do you do?" and "Where are you going?" They are innocent questions intended to be simple ice-breakers to open up a conversation and get to know a new person. For us traveling on this Greatest Expedition, those questions get at the heart of why we exist as Christians and are critical questions for our churches.

This book will focus on the "what," the "why," and the "where" of your new expedition. These three questions are closely connected in ministry. They are also questions too many churches have lost sight of over the years. Pause now and consider these questions from your personal church experience. Think about a specific church where you spent the most amount of time, a church where you were very involved in the leadership aspects of that ministry. This could be a church you are a part of now, or it might be a church from earlier in your ministry life. Now record your answers to these questions:

- What was it that church did?
- Why did that church do what it did?
- Where was that church going?

Now imagine we were somehow able to gather all of the other people who were in leadership in that church you thought of a minute ago, along with all of the other people in the congregation, and those in the mission field around that church, and asked them also to answer each of those same three questions. What do you think those responses would look like? Mostly the same? Lots of consistency, but with different words and phrases? (Hallelujah!) Or do you think everyone would have a different response to each of the questions? Would many people not even be able to answer the questions? That is much more likely in our experience working with churches. Unfortunately, too many people do not know what their church does, why they do it, or where the ministry is going.

In some cases, there are people in the church who feel they know exactly what the church does, but the answer varies from person to person. For example, when asked what their church does, one person might say, "We feed the hungry," another person might say, "We gather to worship God," and someone else might say, "We pray for those who are hurting." All of those are, of course good, they should be seen as outputs of our mission and not the mission itself. This may be the reason so many churches are struggling today. Too often, we are confusing ministry programs or activities with our mission from Christ. Everything starts with mission. So let's see what we can do to put you and your Greatest Expedition Team in a place where you can be fruitful in your ministry!

CHAPTER ONE
Mission

Jesus came near and spoke to them, "I've received all authority in heaven and on earth. Therefore, go and make disciples of all nations, baptizing them in the name of the Father and of the Son and of the Holy Spirit, teaching them to obey everything that I've commanded you. Look, I myself will be with you every day until the end of this present age."

Matthew 28:18-20 (CEB)

Mission is what an organization does. Think about a large organization in your community. What is it that organization does? What is it the school in your community does? How about the hospital, doctor's offices, or other healthcare facilities in the area? What is it they do? What about all the restaurants and retail stores in the community? What is it they do? Take a few minutes now to write down what you think a few of the organizations in your area do, and then go on Google and see if you can find a mission statement on any of those organization's websites. If you find a few, how close was what you wrote to what the organization says that they do? There are times where the people who interact with an organization might have a very different impression of what that organization does than what the leaders of the organization state as their mission.

"The mission of Southwest Airlines is dedication to the highest quality of Customer Service delivered with a sense of warmth, friendliness, individual pride, and Company Spirit." Would you have written that mission for Southwest Airlines if you were a customer? The company certainly hopes you would! Notice how even though the word "airlines" is in their name, nothing about their mission statement is really about air travel. It is not even about travel at all. It is about customer service. In this example, we see a hint of "why," which we will come back to later.

The mission of a business organization impacts at least three major groups of constituents: the employees of that organization; the customers of that organization who purchase products and/or services from that organization; and other organizations who provide supplies in the form of materials and/or services. A wise business will consider at least those three groups when they create a company mission statement.

How about churches? What is it that churches do? If we were to look at your church's website, read your bulletin, talk to your ministry leaders, examine your church newsletter, review your church calendar, and tour your facilities, what might we say is your mission? Would we see your mission statement printed anywhere? If we were to stop people who had just attended a worship service or other gathering at your church and asked them what it was that your church did, what would they say? What would a person who sat in on all your committee meetings say is your church's mission? What would the people who live in the neighborhood around your church say it is that you do?

Go back and reread Matthew 28:18-20 listed above. Do you see our mission there? In simple terms, churches make disciples. That is what we do. That is what Jesus commanded us to do. That is why these verses are known as the Great Commission (and not the great suggestion).

> **"Mission is a broad, brief, biblical statement of what the ministry is supposed to be doing."**
>
> Aubrey Malphurs

Jesus was very specific with his followers. For those of us who continue to follow Jesus, this must be what we do. Until you are clear on the mission, your church will be unable to cast God's vision, set goals, or create objectives in a relevant manner. Each of these areas is tied together, but the mission must be the starting point. The mission is our clear identity. It is connected to our purpose. It is also the key to our "why," which we will get to soon.

In the book *Advanced Strategic Planning,* author and seminary professor Aubrey Malphurs says, "Mission is a broad, brief, biblical statement of what the ministry is supposed to be doing."

The mission states the intention of the congregation. The mission statement should be broad. It is intended to be more general than specific. Mission is a big picture statement. It should be brief. Most mission statements are one sentence. People should be able to remember the full mission statement. Too many words or too long, and people will struggle to recall everything. The mission statement of a church should be biblical. There should be a clear connection to the mission Jesus gave us in Matthew 28:18-20. The mission of a church states the intention of the congregation. No church is perfect at making disciples. There is room for all congregations to improve their disciple-making process. But our purpose must be to make disciples.

> *...the church's mission is to make disciples. Thus, the evaluation of the mission demands, Show me your disciples! In 2 Corinthians 13:5, Paul instructs the church at Corinth, "Examine yourselves to see whether you are in the faith; test yourselves."*
>
> **Aubrey Malphurs, Advanced Strategic Planning**[1]

Jesus was and is very clear. Our mission is to make disciples. Many churches will say

---

[1] Aubrey Malphurs, *Advanced Strategic Planning*. Baker Books. Grand Rapids. 2013.

that in different ways. Some churches over the years have hired people and gotten very creative in how they articulate their mission. That is fine, as long as no matter what we say clearly connects back to Matthew 28:18-20. Some churches have used the mission statement, "To know Him, and make Him known." It is very clever. It is short enough to fit on a tee shirt or wristband. Seven words are short enough for most people to remember. And best of all, it can easily connect back to our mission as stated by Jesus in Matthew 28:18-20.

In The United Methodist Church denomination, the following mission statement is understood and adopted in many local churches. Here is the mission statement of the denomination:

> *The making of disciples of Jesus Christ for the transformation of the world.*
>
> **Mission of The United Methodist Church**

It isn't necessary to spend a lot of time, effort, or resources trying to determine what God calls us to do as a church. The church is a child of God and therefore equipped to be the family of God. There are many service organizations serving people with needs in most communities. However, what is the difference between the church and other service organizations? God! We serve people in the name of God! We serve people out of our love of Jesus Christ and our desire to teach others about the love and grace of Jesus Christ. This is truly taking ownership of our purpose and what makes us unique. Until we grasp that basic understanding and responsibility for being a church, we will meander through the day-to-day "doing church" and not becoming the church with a mission.

> *It is not so much the case that God has a mission for his church in the world, as that God has a church for his mission in the world. Mission was not made for the church; the church was made for mission – God's mission.*
>
> **Christopher J. H. Wright**

The mission is stagnant. The mission (purpose of the church) of an organization does not change, nor does the mission of a church change over time. We don't expect the Great Commission to change anytime soon! So, we believe that until Jesus comes back to tell us otherwise, we need not spend a lot of time trying to determine the mission of our church. Let's do what was said to us in the Great Commission! Unfortunately, too many churches will invest time, energy, and resources to figure out their church's mission when it has already been given to us. Instead, we should embrace the mission provided to us by Jesus and invest our energies living into that mission.

When Jesus says we should "Go make disciples," is he talking about focusing on reaching new people, people who are not currently connected to the church? Is Jesus telling us to go and share our faith story with people so that they will start following him? Is the focus on what we would call "evangelism?" Or is Jesus commanding us to help those who are already followers grow in their faith? Is Jesus telling us that we need to keep growing closer to him? Is the focus on what we would call "sanctification?" We believe the answer is, "YES!" It is our belief that when Jesus said, "Go make disciples," it was not an either/or. It was a both/and command. Our churches, pastors, laity leaders, and all Christians need to focus on growing ourselves and others already in church to take the next step on our spiritual journey AND always be about reaching ONE more lost sheep.

When Jesus tells the parable of the Lost Sheep in Luke, he is sitting with "tax collectors and sinners," and the church people, the Pharisees, were listening.

> *Suppose someone among you had one hundred sheep and lost one of them. Wouldn't he leave the other ninety-nine in the pasture and search for the lost one until he finds it? And when he finds it, he is thrilled and places it on his shoulders. When he arrives home, he calls together his friends and neighbors, saying to them, "Celebrate with me because I've found my lost sheep." In the same way, I tell you, there will be more joy in heaven over one sinner who changes both heart and life than over ninety-nine righteous people who have no need to change their hearts and lives.*
>
> **Luke 15:4-7 (CEB)**

That parable is very tough for many Christians to hear. Those who are not yet mature in their faith will often focus so much on the leaving of the ninety-nine that it makes them think, "What about us? Don't we count?" Notice that Jesus did not say the shepherd left the ninety-nine and went and started a new herd. No, the shepherd brought the lost sheep back home. And then what happened? There was a celebration! Imagine a church where there was a celebration every time a new person was brought home, every time someone took a step on their faith journey, every baptism, every confirmation, and every profession of faith. We sometimes speak of heaven rejoicing during some of these occasions. Why are we not rejoicing with heaven?

For generations, all levels of church leaders have been focusing on how we might best turn around the decline in our churches. We have read and written hundreds of books on how to fix churches. We have attended seminars, hired consultants, bought the latest programs, changed worship styles, and much more, just to find the one secret that will magically grow our churches. The late Rev. Junius B. Dotson, General Secretary/CEO of Discipleship Ministries, says, "Let's stop fixing churches and start seeing the people Christ called us to reach." There is, of course, value in most of the books, seminars, programs, consultants, and overall changes many churches have engaged with over the years.

We are just focusing on the wrong thing.

In the book of Matthew, Chapter 16, Jesus and his disciples are walking along and came to Caesarea Philippi. As is the custom with Jewish rabbis, Jesus asked his followers many questions. In this exchange, Jesus asked, "Who do people say I am?" There were several responses from the group, John the Baptist, Elijah, Jeremiah, or other prophets. Then Jesus makes it personal by asking, "Who do you say I am?" Peter then replies in verse 16, "You are the Christ, the Son of the living God." Jesus then indicates that this response from Peter did not come from his mind but was given to him by God. Most Christians know that story. We have preached it or heard it preached. We have seen it in movies and studied it in classes. However, like many areas of the Bible, we stop too soon. Peter's declaration about Jesus is extraordinary. It deserves our attention. So does verse 18, "I tell you that you are Peter. And I'll build my church on this rock. The gates of the underworld won't be able to stand against it." For generations, we have been trying to build the church. Remove the yoke of building the church from your back. That was never our job! Jesus will build the church. Our job is to make disciples. How did we ever get this so backward?

We have seen examples of this for years. A church focuses on growing, only to end up continuing to decline. Another church focuses on making disciples, and new people just keep showing up. We believe that this is the work of the Holy Spirit. The more a church focuses on its mission to make disciples of Jesus, the more the Holy Spirit says, "Way to go. Here are some more people. Keep up the good work!"

Mike Breen sums this up in his book, *Building a Discipling Culture,* by saying:

> *If you make disciples, you always get the church. But if you make a church, you rarely get disciples.*[2]

Read that again. How different might our world be today if churches had been focusing their time and resources on making disciples?

Many churches and whole denominations have been focusing on the wrong targets. In the past, the main number talked about in the church world was membership. Around the turn of the 21st century, the focus shifted

---

[2] Mike Breen, *Building a Discipling Culture.* 3D Ministries Publishing. 2009.

from membership to worship attendance. To focus on growth, many churches created goals for baptisms, professions of faith, first-time guests, and more. Each year many churches report statistics in a hundred or more areas of church life. All of those are good for us to know as church leaders, but they all make terrible targets. The target is our mission, to make disciples.

In his book, *Doing the Math of Mission: Fruits, Faithfulness, and Metrics,* Gil Rendle makes it clear that we "count so we can measure." We count and keep track of areas like worship attendance not because those are the targets but because they can help us see if we are on the right track to our target/mission to make disciples.

In his book, *Quietly Courageous: Leading the Church in a Changing World,* Rendle takes this even further by showing how data leads us to information that gives us knowledge. Last week's worship attendance, while representing the people of God, is still just a number. When we review a year's worth of worship attendance data, we can often see trends and gain information about the fruitfulness of our discipleship efforts. The data and information should lead us to a knowledge of what we need to do as Christian leaders. The goal of knowledge is to create action. Continuing just to gather data is not helping our ministry or being faithful to God. What are we doing with all this information? What is it telling us about the state of our church? The collection of statistics has become our target. Pause and reread this paragraph before you get too excited and decide to stop counting and reporting everything.

We do need to count. We need to report statistics. But it must lead us to action. We count so that we can gain information about our ministry. We need information to lead us to the knowledge of the correct action we must take for us to be more fruitful in our making of disciples.

In a new faith community like a brand-new church of some form, the leaders will benefit from starting everything with a clean slate. The mission can be established and used to guide all of the church's ministries from the first day. What about in an established church that has been around for years or maybe decades? How can a church with a history of not focusing on the mission best get back on track? The answer is a re-commitment to the mission.

Before we get into this next section, we need to pause for a minute to reflect on grace and forgiveness. In some cases, when we feel that we have not been true to God's mission, we may experience guilt or shame. We hear a voice in our head telling us we have been unfaithful to what Jesus has commanded us to do here on earth. That is not God's voice. If any part of this book causes you to feel guilt, shame, or question your ministry leadership, then set it down and pray. Spend time reflecting on the many Bible verses which speak to grace and forgiveness. Maybe start with Psalm 86:4-5:

> *Make your servant's life happy again because, my Lord, I offer my life to you, because my Lord, you are good and forgiving, full of faithful love for all those who cry out to you.*

Lay any guilt, shame, or other bad feelings at the foot of the cross. The past is done. Let us keep our faces looking forward to God's grace.

A re-commitment to the mission must start with the pastor(s). A few years ago, a pastor was working with a coach. During one of their sessions, the pastor shared her frustration of being pulled in too many different directions. She said that it felt like the congregation had one job description for her, the Staff/Parish Relations team had another job description for her, and the District Superintendent had yet another job description for her. And none of those expectations were aligned with each other, much less what she felt was her job. After a few minutes of venting, the pastor exclaimed, "I don't even know what it is I do!" The coach paused for a moment and then asked, "What do you think it is you are called to do?" They decided to let it sit for a while. They picked up where they left off the next week, and the pastors answered, "I make disciples!" The coach affirmed the pastor's statement, then asked, "How's that going?" For a church to commit to the mission (Matthew 28:18-20), that commitment must start with the pastor(s). Making disciples is not an event. It is not something a pastor or church can focus on for a while and then move on to something else. Every message preached must focus on making disciples. Every newsletter article the pastor writes, every conversation they have, every congregational care visit.

You get the point. Here is a secret that might help. Chances are good. If you are a pastor, you are doing more of this now than you realize. Look at your last few messages. Do you see any parts in those messages about discipleship? Do you see any elements which might help someone who heard the message grow as a disciple? Now, look again. Do you know the word "disciple" or "discipleship" anywhere in your message? (Sorry, referring to someone in the Bible as a disciple does not count.) Discipleship might be the most important, least talked about area of ministry. There are opportunities every day for us to point to areas of ministry and say, "That's discipleship!" Often, we feel it is too obvious to mention. Connecting the dots between actions and behaviors and discipleship can help people understand the concept better.

Once the pastor(s) are clear and committed to the mission to make disciples, the next group to focus on is the church's leadership team. There are many names for this team, the most common is the Administrative Board. No matter what the team/committee is called, we refer to the church's governing body. The group of people must be focused on the overall ministry of the church. For a congregation of any size to really be committed to the Great Commission, the leaders must be modeling and showing the way. Recall the last years' worth of meeting agendas for this team. What does it seem that this team is focusing on now? Our leadership team hears reports of what has already happened in too many churches and focuses on finances, facilities, and putting out fires. We will come back to this leadership team and its agenda when we get to vision. For now, what is most important is for these leaders to be committed to the church's mission to make disciples. (No matter how it is worded or stated.) If this team is currently too buried in the weeds of ministry details to see the big picture, it may take some time and training to move the leaders into a place where discipleship is their primary focus. An excellent resource for your church to use is the book *Mission Possible: A Simple Structure for Missional Effectiveness* by Kay Kotan and Blake Bradford.[3]

---

[3] Kay Kotan and Blake Bradford, *Mission Possible 3+*, Market Square Publishing, 2021.

Your church need not change your overall leadership structure for your leaders to become accountable to our mission.

Once your church's pastor(s) and leadership team are committed to the mission to make disciples, the next group to focus on is your church staff. All churches have a staff. In most churches today, we just do not pay our staff.

Take a few minutes now to list out everyone in your church who is leading some type of ministry (children's ministry, youth, adult education, nursery, worship, music, hospitality, women's, men's, trustees, finance, missions, outreach, etc.). In some cases, those leading an area of ministry were also included in the last area focused on the church's leadership team. Be sure to include them again. One of the most potent conversations you can have with ministry leaders is to clarify the mission of the church and their role in that mission. Invest the time in your ministry to have this conversation with each ministry leader. Here are some key points to guide these conversations:

- One or two people who are already committed to and understand the church's mission should meet with each ministry leader individually. More than one or two people and the ministry leader might feel intimidated. Meeting with each ministry leader individually helps to promote honest and open conversation.

- Spend a few minutes defining the mission and sharing the church's mission statement. Use as much as you need to from this book. Be sure to read and unpack Matthew 28:18-20 during this conversation. Allow the ministry leader to ask questions or make any comments they want to about the mission. Do not assume they know how to define mission or already know the church's mission statement.

- Ask them to share with you how their ministry area helps the church make disciples. No matter how long they have been in this ministry leadership position, this may be the first time anyone has ever asked them that question. Be very aware that this could cause them to feel challenged. Reassure them that you are having this conversation with all ministry leaders to understand better how the church is currently doing with the mission to make disciples and to discern areas where you need to make any adjustments to become more fruitful in the overall ministry.

- Watch and listen for any signs that may

indicate that the ministry leader is feeling guilt or shame about how their ministry has been making disciples. Emphasize a focus more on the future than the past. Stop and pray when you feel it is needed. Remind them of God's love, grace, and forgiveness.

- Spend a few minutes talking about their spiritual journey. Ask them what it would look like to take a step forward on their journey as a disciple this season. Help them identify one spiritual discipline area where they will intentionally focus in the coming weeks or months. Ask what precisely they are going to do differently to grow in that spiritual discipline. Set a day and time for a follow-up conversation about the step they are planning to take. This will model for them what discipleship can look like in a ministry.

- Ask them what resources they may need from you or the church to best support the mission of making disciples. Let them know this is not a one-time conversation. Explain the overall re-commitment to the mission initiative and any potential next steps the church leaders might be planning.

This re-commitment to the mission conversations is intended to work together and support the church's discipleship focus. Being

> "To create fully devoted followers of Jesus Christ, it takes the involvement of each believer and the church to come alongside the work of the Holy Spirit."

committed to the mission of making disciples is only effective if a church has a discipleship process. What is a discipleship process? It is an intentional process that provides the resources and direction for each individual in the church to grow closer to Christ in all spiritual disciplines. The keyword there is "intentional." Discipleship does not happen accidentally. Many people attend church worship services faithfully each week, are involved in a Christian education group, serve in the church or community, pray, and read their Bibles, only to be stuck in the same place on their spiritual journey for years. The Holy Spirit is continually working to move people along on this journey. To create fully devoted followers of Jesus Christ, it takes the involvement of each believer and the church to come alongside the work of the Holy Spirit.

An excellent resource to learn more about this discipleship process is *Stride: Creating a*

Discipleship Pathway for Your Church by Mike Schreiner and Ken Willard.

Having a clear mission that is owned and supported by all church leaders is very important to your ministry for several reasons:

- Mission dictates what it is that your church does. Even churches that are in decline are often doing good things. Leaders in congregations rarely have to say, "Stop doing bad things." Mission helps provide the focus all churches need to be true to the Great Commission.

- Mission provides a foundation upon which your church can build as you do strategic ministry planning. Other components such as vision, goals, core values, and purpose are part of any effective strategic ministry planning process. However, they all build upon a clear mission that is understood and supported by all church leaders.

- Mission formulates the ministry's function. You will never do ministry that matters until you can define what matters. Mission is that expression of strategic intent. All church ministries must be making disciples, which is their function.

- Mission provides a guideline for decision-making. It gives direction for when church leaders should be saying "yes," and when they should be saying "no," or maybe "not right now." All leadership decisions should be held up to the lens of disciple-making. "Will doing this help us make disciples?"

- Mission inspires ministry unity. A clear mission gives all ministries a unifying theme to follow. Instead of each ministry operating in a silo, they can work together under the same focus. An example of this in many churches is the children's ministry and the youth ministry areas. Too often, there is a clear divide between the two. Different people are leading those ministries, and due to the perceived different requirements of each age group, they rarely communicate, much less partner together. When those ministries embrace the mission to make disciples of all ages, they can begin to see how supporting each other can translate into a more seamless transition between the two for the kids, and where they might join their forces together to better help everyone take a step on their spiritual journey.

- Mission facilitates evaluation of ministry effectiveness. The church's mission is to make disciples. When we review a ministry for effectiveness to the mission, they should clearly show how they are helping people grow on their walk to be more like Christ. While this type of evaluation should focus on accountability to the mission, it should not be received as a punitive type of accountability. This is a Christian model of accountability. "You said you were going to do this. How is it going?" This is front-loaded accountability. Explain the process to each ministry ahead of time. This is not a process to catch people doing something wrong.

Mission is one component of determining where the church is on its life cycle. Our effectiveness in the church for making disciples enables us to see which direction we are heading. We will cover the church life cycle in more detail later in the book. For now, it is essential to understand that knowing our mission and being true to that mission of making disciples will usually indicate whether our church is in a growth mode or a decline mode. Next, let's take a look at *purpose,* why our church does what it does.

CHAPTER TWO
Purpose

*Many plans are in a person's mind,
but the Lord's purpose will succeed.*

Proverbs 19:21

We have looked at the "what" element of mission. In the church, mission is what we do. We make disciples. Now we are going to look at the "why" element of purpose. While most churches have some form of mission statement, even if they are just using their denomination's or affiliation's mission statement, very few churches have any form of purpose statement. Before going any further, please understand that the intent of this section is not for you to create a purpose statement. The objective of this section is for you and your church leaders to gain clarity on your purpose. You may choose to create a purpose statement or to put something in writing. There is nothing wrong with that. It is just not the focus of this section.

Purpose comes down to why your church, congregation, ministry exists. Many mission statements in business and church organizations will contain some element of purpose. Remember the mission statement of the United Methodist denomination we shared earlier? "Making disciples of Jesus Christ for the transformation of the world." The first half is all about mission, "making disciples of Jesus Christ." The second half is about purpose, "for the transformation of the world." The purpose explains "why" we are doing the "what." The "what" part is strategic, focusing on our functional job of making disciples. This speaks to our head. It is pragmatic. The "why" part is more emotional, focusing on our calling as a church to change (improve) the world. This speaks to our heart; it is more aspirational. The two work well together.

Look back at the beginning of this book. You were asked to think about a specific church where you spent the most amount of time, a church where you were very involved in the leadership aspects of that ministry. Then answer three questions. The first question was, "What was it that church did?" That's the mission question. The second question was, "Why did that church do what it did?" That's the purpose question. What were your answers to those two questions? Were they reflected in, or at least connected to that church's mission statement?

Mission statements are important. Understanding the mission and having all ministries in the church aligned to and supporting the mission is a whole new level. When those ministry leaders are also clear on why, the purpose, we are doing the mission, this creates a force which even the gates of hell cannot withstand! Think of mission and purpose as two sides of the same coin. They just go best together.

Have you ever been told what to do? Being told what to do will at best produce compliance. Not a bad thing. But God's Kingdom is not about compliance. The Ten Commandments quickly grew to over 600 laws and some of that was due to a focus on compliance. Here is what you must do. Now think about an occasion where someone took the time to explain to you why something needed to be done. It might still be

> "Knowing why something must be done creates commitment."

hard work, but knowing why it needs to be done is freeing for most people. Knowing why something must be done creates commitment. When people are compliant, they will usually focus on the minimum which must be done to get by. Laws, rules, regulations, policies, all focus on making people be compliant. When people are committed, they often go above and beyond what is expected. Committed people don't break laws, rules, regulations, or policies, but their focus is more on following the "why" and less on doing something wrong.

There are different versions of training which focus on this such as The Hierarchy of Commitment or several Commitment Continuums. If you think about a horizontal continuum which goes from left to right the far left might indicate people who are resistant to the mission, they are not bought in at all or maybe they disagree with the church's stated mission. This is usually a very small group if they exist at all, in most churches. The next group to the right could be those who are reluctant to support the mission for some reason. If you are introducing the mission or re-introducing the mission, they may just be taking a wait and see approach. The next group to the right on the continuum are those who are just going through the motions. They know the mission in their head, but it is not in their heart. This group can be dangerous because they may support the mission publicly but then undermine it with their friends privately. The compliant group is next.

As stated before, this is the group that supports the mission, but only does so because that is what they have been told to do. For them it is a law or rule that should not be broken. But that is as far as their support goes. Then we reach the committed group. They are self-motivated about the mission and will go the extra mile. They are excited about making disciples and it shows. The final group on our continuum are those who are compelled. They will not only support the mission, but they will find a way to do so no matter what gets in their way. They will make disciples even if told not to do so. Their spirit is contagious. People are drawn to them and come away fired up about the mission. Our role as leaders is to understand we will likely have people in our congregation at each of these stages and the best way for us to help them take a step closer to becoming committed and compelled to our mission is through a clear communication of why. We cannot push people through this mission continuum, but we can lead forward.

Mission statements get printed on paper. They are painted on the wall in a church facility. They are often prominent on a church's website. The purpose is usually verbal. It is spoken more than it is written. Leaders talk about the purpose to engage people's emotions. Pastors preach on the church's purpose to ignite people's hearts and activate the congregation's calling. There is a very good *Ted Talk* with Simon Sinek called, "How great leaders inspire action." While his talk is focused on the business world, there is some great learning there about the real power of "why." This would be a great video for the whole team to watch together as you work on purpose for your ministry.

Take another look at the mission statement of your church. Is the purpose of the church in that statement somewhere? How would you explain the purpose of your church to a first-time guest? Spend some time with your Expedition Team discussing the purpose of your church. Before we move into the next section where we talk about where God is calling your church, it is important for your whole team to be clear on what you do and why you are doing that.

> *Every church should have a mission statement and a vision statement. The two are inextricably related but are clearly distinct. Mission precedes vision, but without vision, it is empty and incomplete.*
>
> **George Barna, The Power of Vision**[4]

---

[4] George Barna, *The Power of Vision*, Baker Books, 2018.

CHAPTER THREE
Vision

If people can't see what God is doing, they stumble all over themselves; but when they attend to what he reveals, they are most blessed.

Proverbs 29:18 (MSG)

First, we looked at the "what" element of mission. Mission is what an organization does. (Or at least what the organization intends to do.) In the church, our mission is to make disciples. That is very clearly what Jesus commanded us to do. Next, we looked at purpose. Purpose is the "why" element. In the church, purpose explains why we do what we do in our ministry. Why does our church exist? A well-thought-out mission statement will often have elements of purpose. We will now move into the final element for this book of "where," which is all about vision.

Many church leaders are unfamiliar with the distinctions between mission and vision. For that reason, you may often see a church share what is clearly their mission statement and call it their vision. Or vice versa. This book uses simple definitions to clarify how mission is different from vision. On this Greatest Expedition journey, you and your team may need to revisit not just the importance of each element (mission/what; purpose/why; and vision/where), but you may also need to remind yourselves and others of the definitions of each and how they work with and support each other.

Think about all the churches in your community. Go on Google and search for "churches near me." Click on the map and then adjust the size until you have a good view of what you think of as your mission field. See all those churches? Guess what? They all have the same mission as your church! (As long as they are Christian churches.) All churches' mission is to make disciples of Jesus. They may all say it in different ways, or they may not say it, but it is still the same mission. All those churches in your community have a different and unique vision. Each church in your area is made up of different people who have different gifts. Each church is in a different place geographically, even if they are just across the street from each other. Each church has a different history and is in a different and unique reality right now. So while God is calling all churches forward to a new vision, those visions will be unique from each other.

> *Vision is the ability to see God's presence, to perceive God's power, to focus on God's plan in spite of the obstacles.*
>
> **Charles Swindoll**

Vision is a discernment process. Building on the work of Andy Stanley, we will define vision as a clear, concise, compelling, and challenging picture of the future of your church or ministry as you believe that it not only can but must be. Years ago, a church consultant was working with a church where most of the congregation consisted of very well-educated engineers who worked for a government facility nearby. The consultant facilitated one day's workshop on vision and how important it was for the church to focus on where God was calling them to go. During a break, a congregation member approached the consultant and asked, "What's the formula for figuring out our vision?" Unfortunately, there is no formula. Vision is all about discernment. It is about hearing God's voice above all the other voices of our world. There are things we can do to help put us in place to hear better and understand the whisperings of the Holy Spirit, but there is no $X + Y / Z =$ vision. Sorry.

Vision should always have an element of the future. We are not there yet but are heading in that direction. We hear God's voice calling us to a new place through prayer, reading scripture, and engaging with others in the community. If a church is not careful, the vision will be what they want and not necessarily what God wants because they only listen to their voices.

Vision is not necessarily a statement that has to be easily remembered or able to be put on a bumper sticker, tee-shirt, or wristband. Although many times, keywords dominate the statement and can be used as flagship reminders of the statement. These keywords can also name the ministry teams that will lead the congregation into accomplishing the vision. This allows a clear vision connection into the action steps of achieving the vision through the ministries.

In Thom Ranier's book, *Breakout Churches*,[5] he defines the "Vision Intersection Profile." This is an excellent self-discovery tool that allows a church to discern the community's needs, the passions of the church leadership, and the congregation's gifts by using a Venn diagram. For it is where all these three intersect that the vision from God for this congregation lies. The following quote from Andy Stanley's book *Visioneering* may be helpful for you or anyone on your Greatest Expedition Team who is new to the whole vision discernment process. Read the section below and see if it reminds you of times in your ministry where the church or ministry team you were a part of was following a vision, even if it was not stated as such.

> *What is a vision? Where do they come from? Visions are born in the soul of a man or woman who is consumed with the tension between what is and what could be. Anyone*

---

[5] Thom Ranier, *Breakout Churches*, Zondervan, 2010.

who is emotionally involved—frustrated, broken-hearted, maybe even angry—about how things are in light of how they believe things could be is a candidate for a vision. Visions form in the hearts of those who are dissatisfied with the status quo...Vision carries with it a sense of conviction. Anyone with a vision will tell you this is not merely something that could be done. This is something that should be done. 6

> **"Mission creeps, and vision leaks."**

Before we get into what might be considered the practical aspects of vision discernment, there are a few more important aspects of this process for us to understand. There is a phrase that is believed to have originated with the military, "Mission Creeps." The story is that military leaders learned that no matter how clear the mission was at the time of its origin, over time, they would see the mission creep or drift away from that clear path. Conflicting missions or distractions would cause the current mission to look different from the original mission.

---

6 Andy Stanley, *Visioneering*. Multnomah Books. Colorado Springs. 2005.

Sound familiar? That has happened in many churches. If mission creeps, then vision leaks. No matter how great a job you do at casting your vision, you will need to remember that over time that vision will leak out of the minds of your congregation and out of the plans of your leaders. One of the best vision casters in the church world is probably Andy Stanley. He has written books on vision and consults with many churches and businesses about creating and casting vision. Pastor Andy tells the story of being frustrated that he has to preach on his church's vision every year in January. But he has learned that no matter how clear the vision seems at the beginning of the year, it will leak away some by the end of the year.

"Three primary obstacles to making vision stick are success, failure, and everything in-between." Andy Stanley

Unless you are discerning a vision for a brand new church, you will need to be aware of the church's history. God's vision for your church is not going to be about going back to the past. However, the church's past is what many people in your congregation will remember fondly and, on some level, want to return to those great days of the past, even if the reality is they were not so great days. For that reason, it may be helpful to think about the church's history like a book.

This book has many chapters. Some chapters are focused on people, leaders, and pastors. Some chapters focus on significant events that impacted the church, such as wars, changes in population, a four-lane highway coming through the town, a significant industry opening or closing, etc. The vision process is not about writing a new book. Discerning God's vision for the church will lead to the next chapter in the book of the church.

There are usually four stages to the vision discernment process. The first stage is the Prayer & Information stage and usually lasts from six to twelve months. Because vision is a discernment process, we must always focus first on prayer. While prayer is often described as a conversation with God, vision discernment must focus more on the listening to God aspect and less on the speaking to God part of the conversation. As you and your team are spending time in prayer and reading scripture, be sure to record what you are hearing and sensing from God's Spirit. These words, phrases, and images will often be clues to the final vision for your ministry.

We encourage your team to also prayer walk the community around your church to see what God sees concerning the mission field and hear what the Holy Spirit might be whispering to you about the people you have been called to serve. You might start with your Expedition Team or maybe the leadership team of the church. Pair up everyone and ask them to spend twenty to thirty minutes walking the streets around your church facility. Encourage them to lift up prayers for everyone they see and whenever the Spirit moves them. For example, if they pass a school, they could pray for the students, pray for the teachers, and pray for all of those on the support staff. The prayers should not be spoken aloud, and anyone who sees them should just think they are out for a walk. Most of their time should be spent quietly listening and observing what God is saying and showing them.

The most important part of prayer walking is the debrief time where everyone can share what they heard and saw, which they feel was from God. For more information on prayer walking, read the book *Stride: Creating a Discipleship Pathway for Your Church* by Mike Schreiner and Ken Willard.

Here are some other important elements for you to do during the Prayer & Information stage of your vision discernment process:

- Read a few books on strategic ministry planning and/or vision. There is a listing in the back of this book of a few books we recommend. The books, S*trategy Matters: Your Roadmap for an Effective Ministry Planning Retreat* by Kay Kotan and Ken Willard and *God Dreams: 12 Vision Templates for Finding and Focusing Your Church's Future* by Will Mancini and Warren Bird are two we would suggest you start with to give you a strong foundation for this journey.

- Complete the Church Self Study found in the appendix of this book. The purpose of that tool is to give you a clear picture of where the church has been and where it is right now. This image of the current realities both inside the church and in the community will better enable you to hear where God is calling you to go.

- Create urgency in the congregation. As you begin to share your findings and accurately describe the current reality in the ministry, emphasize why we cannot stay where we are now. This will create some tension in the congregation. Do not eliminate it, but use it to start focusing people toward the future.

- Facilitate focus groups with influential people and groups in your congregation who are not part of your Greatest Expedition Team. Here are some suggested questions for you to ask these groups:

  - What is going well in our church? What is the best thing about our church? Where do we see fruit? [What do we need to grow, optimize, amplify?]

  - What is not going as well as it should and/or as well as we would like in our church? [fix/stop] What needs to change? What is holding us back?

  - What is missing? [add]

  - What is confusing? What does not fit anymore? What do new people find confusing? [clarify]

  - What are we not willing to change?

  - What have been the historical turning points in our church?

  - What makes our church unique?

- What is the role of our pastor?
- What are the potential ceilings to our growth? [parking, worship space, leadership, technology, facilities, pastoral care, scarcity thinking, etc.]

As you are completing each element of this first stage of Prayer & Information in the vision discernment process, you should be considering the second stage of Clarification. This is the stage where everything from stage one gets refined down to just a few key words, phrases, and images. The Clarification stage will usually last several months. The intention is not for you to finish stage one before moving to stage two. There should be a lot of overlap between the two stages.

Imagine your team will use a very large conference room with floor-to-ceiling magnetic whiteboards as your "command center" for the final discernment process. As each piece of the stage one Prayer & Information is completed, it is added to the walls in this room. There are post-it notes from people who went on prayer walks, key learnings from the MissionInsite reports about the mission field, highlights and trends from the community interviews, images from the church's history, a page with the church's mission statement and core values, notes from the focus group conversations, Bible verses people have felt called to submit, key learnings from books the team has been reading, graphs and charts of church statistics for the past twenty years, and more. The whole room ends up covered with the story of where the church has been and where it is now. As the team sits, stands, and kneels in the room over the course of several months, you allow the Holy Spirit to speak to you—God's vision for your church will start to take shape. No, you will likely not see a burning bush, but don't rule it out! What tends to happen is that you begin to see threads of connection and themes emerging from all of the information. A word or image is repeated over and over. God's Spirit is whispering where God is calling the church to go. This discernment process cannot and should not be rushed. It will take the time it takes. God is speaking! We just need to be in a position to hear. God is not hiding the vision for your church from you, but sometimes it seems that way when the other noises around us are too loud.

While God may use the pastor or another ministry leader to cast the vision, discernment should not be done by only one person. Vision discernment takes intentionality and a team. When one person does vision discernment, it tends to be more about what that person wants for the church and not about what God wants for the church.

While God may use the pastor or another ministry leader as the one to cast the vision, discernment should not be done by only one person. Vision discernment takes intentionality and a team. When vision discernment is done by one person, it tends to be more about what that person wants for the church and not as much about what God wants for the church.

Imagine a church that had experienced many years of steady growth. Every few years, they had added on to their facility's new rooms or even a new wing. Without any official policy or decision, each new room or wing had been painted off white. One day the Administrative Board was going to meet to decide about adding on several new rooms in the Children's Ministry wing. They felt it was time to talk about paint colors for those rooms and the whole church. Each member of the church staff's office was painted off white. All the hallways, Sunday school rooms, and even the conference room where they were going to meet were painted off white. A few years ago, a local home improvement store had a big sale on paint, and the church purchased a dozen 50-gallon buckets of off white paint they kept in the basement. Even though God's Spirit might be whispering "Purple Paradise" for the new kids' rooms, it will be hard for anyone on the board to hear that with so much off white speaking to them so loudly. During this stage of the vision discernment process, we need to be very aware of the influence we may be hearing from our voices and the voices all around us.

The next element of the Clarification stage is for your team to begin to draft the vision statement. This draft will be based on everything you have discerned so far. You and your team may find it helpful to research some vision statements from other churches. Be careful not to let them influence you too much. Remember that they are just samples to guide you, not to copy. Many churches have never completed a vision discernment process, and since vision is typically more internal than external item, it may be challenging to find on some church websites. Here is a couple we like:

Here are a couple we like:

- *God has uniquely called us a church planting center where planters and teams are developed to reach the Inland Empire and beyond. Over the next five years, we envision three new daughter churches birthed from our body, which will become parenting churches. We will raise and release the next generation of leaders needed for a post-modern world.*
– Mount Calvary Church

- *God has called Morning Star Church to be a WELL, where imperfect people inside and outside the church are REFRESHED, RESTORED, and RESOURCED to enrich their relationships with God, self, and others. And intentionally REACH ONE MORE for Jesus!*
– Morning Star Church

Typically, this process of drafting a vision statement will take several times of going back and forth between the members of your team and other key leaders in the church with time for prayer and discernment. There are several things to watch out for as you are drafting this new vision statement. Be careful the statement is not too vague. Some vision statements are not distinctive enough, and they end up so broad that they could be used at any church. Don't use too many superlatives to focus on the destination God is calling the church. The vision statement should be motivating, not bland. The annual goals of the church should fit nicely under the vision statement.

The final element of the Clarification stage is creating a communication plan. This will be your plan to cast the vision to your whole church. Do not wait until you have a final vision statement to begin working on the communication plan. Work with the person or people in your church responsible for communications to start creating a plan as soon as possible. Consider your church calendar, holidays, and other events when determining the best time to share the vision publicly.

The third stage of the vision discernment process is Casting the Vision. In this stage, you are sharing the church's vision with others outside your team. The specific elements of this stage will be based on the communications plan you created in the Clarification stage. You will be creating awareness of the new vision and what it means to the entire congregation. Care should be taken to connect your church's mission, vision, and values. Everyone needs to see the differences and how they interact and support each other. You do not want people to feel like this is somehow the "flavor-of-the-month," and the mission and values are being replaced. Here are a few best practices for this stage:

- Preach a sermon series on the elements of ministry strategic planning: mission, vision, values, and goals. End the series with vision so you can make your new vision a major reveal. Depending on your vision statement, the vision portion of the sermon series may be delivered through multiple sermons. As you preach on each of the four elements, share examples from the Bible, share what each component looks like for individuals, and then focus on what that element looks like in your church.

- The day or two before you reveal the new vision to the whole congregation, hold a special vision night for your leaders. Make it a party. During the Vision Night, share an overview of how the team discerned this new vision and what it will mean for the future of your ministry. Give time for leaders to ask questions.

The fourth and final stage of the vision discernment process is the Own It stage. For any new vision to stick, the whole church must own it. This starts with the pastor and leaders. To own the vision, it must be used to make ministry decisions. The church leaders should create annual SMARTER goals which will empower the church to move toward this God-breathed vision. (See the book *Time Management for Christian Leaders* by Ken Willard for setting SMARTER goals.)

The pastor and members of the Greatest Expedition Team will need to work with all other church leaders and staff, paid and unpaid, to understand how this new vision impacts their ministry. Care should be taken not to miss any person or ministry. Otherwise, it could give the impression that they can just continue as they have been doing in the past. The new vision must have some impact on each person/ministry in the church. Your goal is for the mission and vision to become part of your church's DNA. This means that each meeting should include a time to review and discuss the mission and vision of the church. When it feels like you have said it too much, you have probably reached about 15% of the congregation. Plans should also be put in place to recast the vision at least annually intentionally.

CHAPTER FOUR
Church Life Cycle

We will end this book about the *what, why,* and *where* of the New Expedition with a discussion of church life cycles. This is based on the work of author and church consultant Rev. George Bullard. If you go on Google and search "George Bullard church life cycle," then click on "images," you will see many examples of what a church life cycle might look like.

Like people, churches have a life cycle. They are born, mature, and someday they reach the end of their life cycle and die. The good news is that churches can have multiple life cycles! While it is true that most congregations do not fit neatly into one of Bullard's categories, we should note that there is usually one stage that predominates and enables a church to determine its current position in the life cycle.

In the classic Bullard life cycle, four areas influence where a church is on the life cycle. The four areas are:

- Vision – which may also include factors such as mission, purpose, values, and leadership
- Relationships – which may also include factors such as discipleship and the experiences of the congregation
- Programs – also known as ministries – may also include factors such as events, services, and activities
- Management – also known as structure – may include systems, accountability, and resources.

Imagine a car that has two seats in the front and two seats in the back. You have four adults who need to fit into the car. Their names are vision, relationships, programs, and management. Where they are sitting will impact the car's travel towards its destination. A major factor is who is driving!

When vision and relationships drive a congregation's agenda, the church tends to be on the upward side of the life cycle. The church is usually experiencing growth of some type

> "Churches can have multiple life cycles."

and fruitful ministry. When programs and management control the agenda, the church tends to be on the downward side of the life cycle. The church is usually turning inward and feels that its best days are in the past. All these elements are good and necessary in all churches. The important distinction is to be aware of who is driving.

Leaders in the church should focus more on "both/and" and less on "either/or" as they learn to manage the polarities in the congregations. The church needs a fresh vision for the future from God – and should always honor the past and those who got us here today. We must prioritize relationships that embrace new people, make them feel welcome, and continue to grow those who are here as disciples.

Our church programs must focus on outreach beyond our building walls – and we need ministries focused on discipleship. The management or structure of our church must be anchored in Christian accountability AND trust that God will guide and provide for us on our journey toward God's preferred future for our church and us.

AFTERWORD
Leadership is Hard Work

Clarifying a church vision is like carving a statue. You start with a massive block of stone and cut away all that doesn't belong to the final product.

You trim away the excess, anything that prevents the statue from having all the lines and clarity you want. Finally, the statue is left, much smaller than the original block, but communicating much more at the same time.

Author Unknown

This is hard work. Leadership in the church today is more challenging than ever. Our country and the world have been through a major pandemic, most of our churches in the United States are either plateaued or in decline, and many of our congregations are aging at a rapid rate. There is no need to go on with this list. You know the church situation as well as anyone. The point here is that it is easy for pastors and church leaders to focus all of their time and effort on just keeping their head above the water that they lose sight of what is important.

Our prayer is that you have discovered or maybe rediscovered the importance and power of mission, purpose, and vision through this book. There is no magic wand. There is no church consultant secret anyone can share with you, which will suddenly turn things around in your ministry or cause your struggling church to start growing. However, a commitment to God's mission of making disciples and a clear vision of where God is calling a church to go has shown over and over again to create more vitality in congregations and more fruitful ministries. We have seen it. You can do it. The investment you make today concerning your church's mission, purpose, and vision will bring fruit for years to come.

We encourage you to use the self-study at the back of this book as a tool to begin this process. Your Greatest Expedition Team is a perfect group to divide up the self-study and complete each section over several weeks. As mentioned earlier in the book, think about each component of the self-study being hung on the wall in a room in your church. As your team reads the pages, prays, and discerns, you begin to hear God's vision. This will grow upon your work concerning mission and purpose. Here are a few final points:

- Keep pulling those three elements together because, in our experience, they too often get separated. Hopefully, you see now the clear connections between mission, purpose, and vision. Help others see those connections too

- Find ways to celebrate what God is doing throughout this process. This is not "work" to be accomplished. It is our way of getting in touch with what God is already doing. Make it a joyful experience.

- Watch out for this becoming a checklist. Having a mission is not the point. It is about doing the mission. Having a vision is also not the point. Living into and moving toward God's vision is what we are called to do.

May God bless you and your team on this

journey as you equip leaders, make disciples, and reach ONE more for God's Kingdom.

APPENDIX
Additional Books

The following are books to assist in learning more about mission, vision, and strategic ministry planning:

Strategy Matters: Your Roadmap for an Effective Ministry Planning Retreat
by Kay Kotan and Ken Willard

God Dreams: 12 Vision Templates for Finding and Focusing Your Church's Future
by Will Mancini and Warren Bird

Advanced Strategic Planning: A New Model for Church and Ministry Leaders by Aubrey Malphurs

Church Unique: How Missional Leaders Cast Vision, Capture Culture, and Create Movement
by Will Mancini

From Values to Action: The Four Principles of Values-Based Leadership
by Harry M. Jansen Kraemer Jr.

Leading Congregational Change: A Practical Guide for the Transformational Journey
by Jim Herrington, Mike Bonem, and James H. Furr

Making Vision Stick
by Andy Stanley

Strategic Thinking: How to Sustain Effective Ministry
by Thomas G. Bandy

The 4 Disciplines of Execution: Achieving Your Wildly Important Goals
by Chris McChesney, Sean Covey, and Jim Huling

The Power of Vision: Discover and Apply God's Plan for Your Life and Ministry by George Barna

Time Management for the Christian Leader
by Ken Willard

Turning Vision into Action
by George Barna

Visioneering: God's Blueprint for Developing and Maintaining Vision

by Andy Stanley

APPENDIX
Church Self-Study

Instructions

1. Gather a team to complete this local church self-study. Those leaders who are part of the Greatest Expedition Team should make up the majority of this team. While the pastor can and should be a part of this process, they should not do all the work themselves. Gathering the information is part of the learning process.

2. As each part of the self-study is divided among the team, give them clear deadlines for completion and where they should go with questions.

3. Once all self-study areas are completed and returned, make arrangements to share the entire package with the retreat participants. In our experience, most churches can

complete the whole self-study in three to four months. This allows for time to pull all parts back together and then share the information with the team.

4. While this self-study may focus on data, statistics, numbers, and information, that should not mean anyone should "turn off God" during the process. We encourage you to make this whole work a prayerful, Spirit-filled process. Each person completing their part of the self-study should be encouraged to spend time in God's Word and prayer before, during, and after completing their assigned section.

Section One – History

Read Acts chapter 2. Pentecost is often referred to as the "birth of the church." What stands out to you about these verses? What do phrases such as "they were all together in one place," or "He poured out this Spirit," or "The Lord added daily to the community" mean to your ministry today?

1. Write a brief history of the congregation. (one-page front and back max) Be sure to include the origin story of the church. Include those events that contributed to

periods of growth or decline in attendance. Write in a factual style, avoiding the temptation to exaggerate information or inject personal commentary. (This should not focus on facilities, but mostly on church ministry.)

2. What are the significant conflicts the church has seen in the past? How would you describe the current state of those conflicts? What, if anything, needs to be done now to resolve any current church conflicts?

3. List dates and provide descriptions for any building construction, major renovations, land acquisitions, or facilities leasing. List the amount of acreage the church owns, leases or rents, the square footage of all buildings, including homes/parsonage.

4. List any formal ties or major connections to other congregations, organizations, or associations. State how the congregation views and interacts with these groups.

5. Provide a listing of all full and part-time paid program staff positions, including pastors, for the last twenty years. Give the dates of tenure and state the reason why they left, if permissible.

6. Provide a list of all people who currently oversee specific areas of ministry. These may be paid positions, but in many churches, they will be unpaid positions. Create an organizational chart that reflects your current structure. Be sure all committees, ministries, teams, groups, and anything else pertinent to this process are included.

Section Two – Statistics

Read Matthew 14:13-21; Mark 8:1-10; and Numbers 1:2

People matter to God. We count people because people count. The Bible is full of statistics and numbers. We tend to see them only as numbers, and too many churches and Christians have developed a fear of data. Every number is important to God because they represent people! Facts are our friends. How do you feel about numbers and statistics? Pray to God now to open you up to see what the Lord sees. (The first two areas of the following are specifically for United Methodist Churches. If your church is not UMC, you will need to find other resources to gather this information. But please do not skip this section.)

1. For United Methodist Churches, go to the website www.umdata.org. Click on the button that says, "STATS." Click on the "Charges/Churches" option listed on the left. Select your jurisdiction, select your conference, and select your district. Locate the name of your church on the list and click on it. At the bottom of the Charts section on the left side of the page is a button that says, "Healthy Church Initiative Download" click

on that button, and an Excel workbook will download, which you can name and save to your computer. This file will give you information your church has submitted for year-end statistics over the last twenty or more years. For other churches, collecting twenty years of data relating to average worship attendance, professions of faith, number of people participating in small groups, number of people involved in the hands-on mission, and generosity.

2. Using this information, create two charts based on the yearly statistics. Go back as far as possible and be sure to include last year, even if it has not been added to this file. One chart should show average attendance and membership for each year. The second chart should include total professions of faith, removed by death, and total baptisms.

3. Estimate the median age of people participating in regularly scheduled worship services in your church. Explain how you came up with this number.

4. State the percentage of people who attend your worship services and attend some form of Christian community (Sunday school, small group meetings, Celebrate Recovery,

other support groups, etc.). Count each individual only once.

5. Prepare a list of the number of current members of your church, or regular attenders, who got involved in your church:

   a. Before 1980
   b. From 1980 to 1989
   c. From 1990 to 1999
   d. From 2000 to 2009
   e. From 2010 to 2019
   f. From 2020 to present.

6. Without listing names state the amount given by each of the top ten contributors on record in the last fiscal year. Total these amounts and state the percentage of giving this represents in relation to the total of all contributions.

7. State the same information as above for the next ten contributors on record.

8. State the total number of contributors to the church during the last fiscal year and the average amount given per contributor.

9. What percentage of the annual budget is going to pay off debt? (mortgage payment, etc.)

Section Three – Community Study

For where two or three are gathered in my name, I'm there with them.

Jesus, Matthew 18:20

1. Write a brief overview of the area and community in which the church building is located and where you primarily serve. (Typically, this is one to two miles around the main church building.)

2. Community Leader Interviews – speak with at least five different key leaders in your community. Examples include but are not limited to *police chief, fire chief, school principal business leader, social worker, school counselor, mayor* or other government officials, chamber of commerce president. The objective here is to gain a new perspective on your mission field. Honor the time of the person you are speaking with by limiting your conversation to thirty minutes or less. Share the following with the person you are interviewing, in your own words:

"Our church is talking to community leaders such as yourself to understand better the community we feel God has called us to serve. Thank you for taking the time to speak with me today. I just have a few questions to ask. I'm going to take notes as we talk so we can compile all of our interviews."

a. Based on your position in our community, what do you see as the top two or three needs of our community?

b. From your unique perspective, what do you know about our community that others might not know?

c. What would you like to see a local church do to improve our community?

d. What would you like to share with our church about this community?

e. From your perspective, what is (your church name) known for in the community?

Thank them again for their time. Once all of the interviews have been completed, compile the notes together by question. Identify any trends you see. Highlight comments to support those trends.

Section Four – Demographics

To complete this section of the self-study, you will need to have access to and a basic understanding of the MissionInsite online system. All United Methodist churches have access to this system through their conference. If you are not part of the United Methodist Church, you can still access this data through MissionInsite.com. You will just need to pay the fee to join first. Similar reports are also available through Gloo.us.

1. Log into MissionInsite.com and go to the *People Plot* section. If you have not already done so, watch the video on how to upload people in your church into the MissionInsite system and upload the Excel sheet as instructed.

    a. Choose your church from the dropdown list on the next page, "Let's Decide Which Congregants You Want to Plot," and click "Next."

b. On the "Now, Let's Decide How the Plots Should be Color Coded" page, leave the "Legend By..." section on "None" and check the box "Show Labels" and then click "Next."

c. On the "Review and Summary" page, click on "Finish."

d. Zoom in on the map on the next page until you see your church building and the names of people in your congregation.

e. On the left side of the page, you should see an icon of a pen called "Draw New Shape and Query" when you click on it, you will be able to create a shape around where the majority of your congregation lives. IMPORTANT NOTES: (1) Try to keep your church in the approximate center of the shape; (2) Try to include most, but not all, of your congregation in the shape. It is common for some people to drive further than others to attend church. Keep your focus close to the building while working to include at least 80% of your worshiping congregation; (3) Do not forget to close the shape by connecting the last point with the first point. (4) If most of the people who are now attending the church do not live in the neighborhood(s) surrounding the church, take note. Discuss this discovery with your team. Why is it that we are not reaching our neighborhood?

   f. Once you have your shape, click on the "demographics" button at the bottom of the page. On the far right, you will now see a "Demographics" section under "Predefined" click on the dropdown next to "Select a predefined report." Be sure to click on your shape, so you are not running reports for a larger area. You will know because your shape will be shown on the first page of the report.

2. Run the following reports: Executive Insite, Comparative Insite, Ministry Insite Priorities, and Religious Insite Priorities.

   a. Print a copy of each report. (double-sided and in color if possible) Save a copy of each report in case you need to print them again.

   b. As you are reviewing all of the information contained within these reports, be sure to answer these questions concerning your mission field (the area of the shape you created):

- What is the total population? Is that population growing, declining, or staying flat over the past years? How does your church's worship attendance trend compare to the population trend?

- What are the racial-ethnic trends? Does your congregation represent your mission field racially?

- What is the average age of your mission field? How does that compare to your church?

- What is the average household income?

- What percentage of households with children are single-parent homes? How does your church minister with single parents?

- What are the percentages of white to blue-collar? How does that compare to your church?

- What are the percentages of each generation in your mission field? How does that compare to your congregation?

- What percentage of people in your mission field are NOT active in a religious congregation or community? How is your church reaching out to these people?

- What "Mosaic Segments" in your mission field is the church reaching now? Which ones does the church need to focus on reaching?

- What percentage of the church's potential giving is the church currently receiving?

3. What are the top three to five things you learned from these reports which should influence how the church does ministry in the next few years?

Section Five – Documents

The Lord replied, "Who are the faithful and wise managers whom the master will put in charge of his household servants, to give them their food at the proper time? Happy are the servants whom the master finds fulfilling their responsibilities when he comes. I assure you that the master will put them in charge of all his possessions."

Luke 12:42-44

1. Gather the following documents or their equivalents:

   a. Last two year's charge conference reports, focusing on what the church has accomplished in ministry during the past two years.

   b. Last two annual budgets and complete financial statements for the past two fiscal years, as well as the most recent financial report for this current year. Be sure to include budget versus actual and balance sheets.

   c. Sample bulletins and newsletters for several seasons if possible, gather at least six of each.

   d. Any policy statements or policy manuals.

   e. Other printed documents or printouts of online information you feel would help provide insight into the church.

Ask at least three people to review this collection of church documents. They do not need to be financial experts or church leaders.

It might be better for them to represent the church's "average" member or attender. In reviewing all these documents:

- What words or phrases often seem to come up?

- What do they indicate is most important to the church?

- What surprises you?

Section Six – Discipleship

Therefore, go and make disciples of all nations, baptizing them in the name of the Father and of the Son and of the Holy Spirit, teaching them to obey everything that I've commanded you. Look, I myself will be with you every day until the end of this present age.

Matthew 28:19-20

1. What is the church's intentional process for growing disciples?

2. What indicators have you seen that this discipleship process is producing fruit?

3. How does a new-to-this-church person get engaged with the discipleship process?

4. What are the church's next steps in the area of discipleship?

Section Seven – Questionnaire

A best practice is to assemble a team of four people to complete the following questionnaire together. This team would have a representative from trustees, finance, hospitality, and children's ministry. The intention is to complete the entire document together and present their findings with any supporting information, then back to the appropriate person coordinating the comprehensive self-study.

1. How many parking spaces are available for each worship service?

    Does the church have enough off-street parking spaces to accommodate at least 80 percent of your average worship attendance?

    How many parking spaces have signs designating them as Handicap?

First-time Guest?

New/Expecting mother?

Others?

2. How many adult Sunday school classes does the church currently have in place?

   Small groups?

   Support or recovery groups?

   Are any of these larger than fifteen people?

   When was the last time the church started a new adult Sunday school class or small group?

3. What is the total capacity of the sanctuary or main worship space? (If using pews, measure the actual pew length and divide by 24 inches.)

   What is 80 percent of total capacity?

   How does that compare to the church's current average worship attendance?

4. What is the total capacity of the nursery? How often is the nursery at capacity during a worship service?

Are infants and toddlers separated?

Is nursery available for all church events?

Are you using Safe Sanctuary guidelines?

Is the church compliant with all Safe Sanctuary guidelines, including having uncovered glass windows in all doors?

How often are toys cleaned?

How often are toys replaced?

What is the church's plan for children in case of an emergency?

What type of check-in system is the church using?

What is the procedure for checking a child into the ministry area for the first time?

How are children with food allergies or other medical issues kept safe?

Are the public schools in the area growing, stable, or declining? (Have data to support your conclusion.)

How many children, on average, are in each ministry room each week?

What is the church's children-to-adults ratio overall?

How are children in the church being grown as a disciple?

5. What days of the week and what hours does the church offer worship each week?

   How were those days and times chosen?

   When was the last time the church changed the number of worship services and/or the worship times?

   How would you describe the types of service and music being offered at each worship? (Using words and phrases a non-church-going person would understand. The words "traditional" and "contemporary" do not mean anything to people outside the church.)

6. Is there an adequate/attractive sign perpendicular to the street with worship times visible (can you read them from a car driving the speed limit) to inform new guests?

   Is there signing from the parking area(s) directing new guests to the right entrance door?

   Are there clear/attractive signs inside the building to help new guests find their way (most important areas: nursery, restrooms, and worship space)?

7. How many first-time guest families does the church average each week? (A good rule is the total number of new-here, first-time guests per year should be equal to or higher than the average number attending worship.)

   How many guests return for a second visit?

   What is the connection system to know who is a first-time guest each week?
   What do first-time guests receive from the church on that initial visit?

   How and when are those new guests contacted?

8. What is the church's process for becoming a member?

   How are people trained and equipped to serve in ministry at the church?

   How many people are involved in serving at the church each week?

   What percentage is that to the average in worship?

   How many people served for the first time last year?

9. What is the church's process for becoming a ministry leader?

   How are people trained and equipped to lead a ministry?

   What is the church's plan to grow both its current leaders and new leaders?

Section Eight – Leadership Questions

Do nothing out of selfish ambition or vain conceit, but in humility, consider others better than yourselves. Each of you should look not only to your own interests, but also to the interests of others.

Philippians 2:3-4

Once you have completed all the previous questions and gathered all of the necessary documents and information, pull it together in a binder or some other form so you can share copies with each person on the team. Give everyone some time to review and process the information, at least 30 days.

Ask them to pray for God's Spirit to give them discernment and wisdom as they study the package of information. After a careful review of the total self-study package, each team member needs to answer the following questions:

- What are the top five strengths of this congregation in priority order?

- What are the two or three most significant challenges/areas of weakness we need to address in the next year to year-and-a-half?

- What do we need to change soon to reach our mission field best and make disciples of Jesus?

- What should NOT change?

- Do you want to see this congregation grow significantly in the next five years?
  Why or why not?

- Are you willing to make the difficult decisions required for change and growth?

  Are you ready to set aside personal preferences to do what the church leaders feel is best for God's Kingdom?

Acknowledgments

All of us working in the church world today stand on the shoulders of those who came before us. There are countless church consultants, authors, leaders and friends who I've had the privilege and honor to work alongside and learn from over the years. People such as:

- George Bullard
- Aubrey Malphurs
- Bob Farr
- Kay Kotan
- David Hyatt
- John Ewart
- Paul Borden
- Gary McIntosh
- Lyle Schaller
- Bill Easum
- Bob Whitesel
- Thom Rainer
- Jim Barber
- and many others

I would like to thank everyone who has helped me on this journey to equip God's people to expand God's Kingdom.

Quotes From Other Books
in The Greatest Expedition Series

The multi-site movement keeps the church centered on God's consistent call to go and make disciples for the transformation of the world while staying connected to one another in community.

Ken Nash
Multi-Site Ministry

Stay flexible even when it is not easy. Due to the stress and responsibility of ministry, we can become rigid, pessimistic and fail to see the opportunities in front of us. A mark of great leadership is flexibility, being able to make adjustments when necessary.

Olu Brown
New Kind of Venture Leader

But let me be clear, we will not be making the case that online relationships and connections are the same as in-person ones; we all know they are not. But we will be talking about why online connections are valuable, and there is nothing "virtual" or "almost" about them.

Nicole Reilley
Digital Ministry

Quotes From Other Books
in The Greatest Expedition Series

While we find struggling churches in different contexts, theological backgrounds, sizes, and cultures, declining congregations have one thing in common: There is a palpable lack of focus on what God desires.

Jaye Johnson
Missional Accountability

How you think of your church will determine not only your priorities, but also your energy investment and actions. It will define how you lead and to what extent you live into what the church of Jesus Christ is intended to be.

Sue Nilson Kibbey
Open Road

Any collaboration with local people is a good thing – but the best collaboration is spiritual. It is where we begin to pray together about the community, and the emerging ministry. In such a spiritual collaboration, amazing things begin to happen.

Paul Nixon
Cultural Competency

What is *The Greatest Expedition*?

The Greatest Expedition is a congregational journey for churches, charges, or cooperative parishes led by a church Expedition Team of 8-12 brave pioneering leaders. The purpose of *The Greatest Expedition* is to provide an experience for Expedition Teams to explore their local context in new ways to develop new MAPS (ministry action plans) so you are more relevant and contextual to reach new people in your community. Updated tools and guides are provided for the church's Expedition Team. Yet, it is a "choose your own adventure" type of journey.

The tools and guides will be provided, but it is up to the church's Expedition Team to decide which tools are needed, which tools just need sharpening, which tools can stay in their backpack to use at a later time, what pathways to explore, and what pathways to pass.

The Greatest Expedition provides a new lens and updated tools to help your Expedition Team explore and think about being the church in different ways. Will your Expedition Team need to clear the overgrown brush from a once known trail, but not recently traveled? Or will the Expedition Team need to cut a brand new trail with their new tools? Or perhaps, will the Team decide they need to move to a completely fresh terrain and begin breaking ground for something brand new in a foreign climate?

Registration is open and Expedition Teams are launching!

greatestexpedition.com

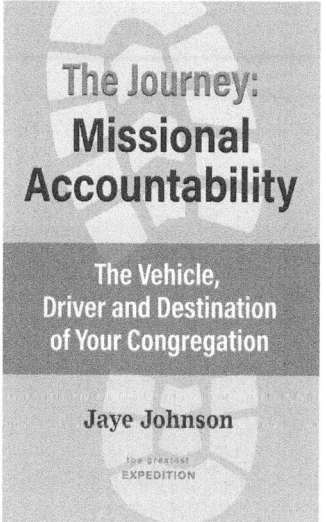

MarketSquareBooks.com

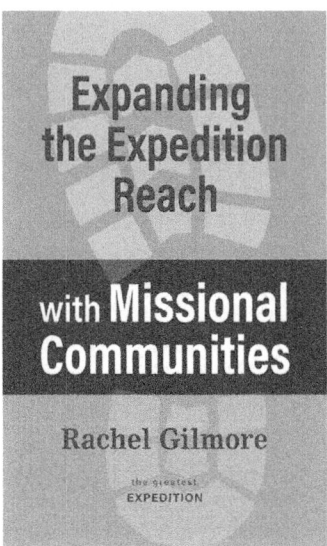
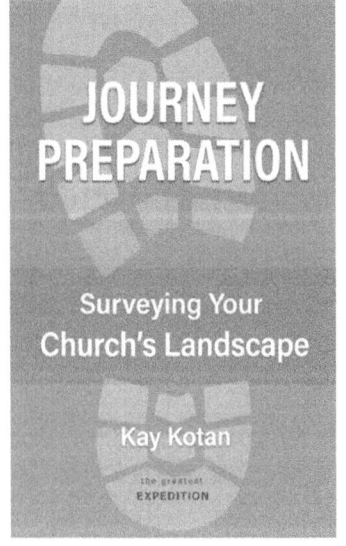

MarketSquareBooks.com

MarketSquareBooks.com

MarketSquareBooks.com

Church Ecology

Creating a Leadership Pathway for Your Church

Ken Willard & Kelly Brown

Introduction by Bishop Sandra Steiner Ball

MarketSquareBooks.com

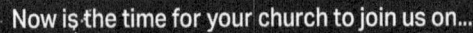

Made in the USA
Monee, IL
04 October 2021